CUSTOMER SERVICE FOR BUISNESS SUCCESS

DON'T LOVE YOUR PRODUCTS MORE THAN YOUR CUSTOMER

AWELE ONWUKA

Copyright © 2024 AWELE ONWUKA

All rights reserved

The characters and events portrayed in this book are fictitious. Any similarity to real persons, living or dead, is coincidental and not intended by the author.

No part of this book may be reproduced, or stored in a retrieval system, or transmitted in any form or by any means, electronic, mechanical, photocopying, recording, or otherwise, without express written permission of the publisher.

ISBN-13: 9798344474113
ISBN-10: 9798344474113

Cover design by: Art Painter
Library of Congress Control Number: 2018675309
Printed in the United States of America

*To God the alimighty, the creator of heaven and earth.
To those who grow humanity through service.
To my family for their encouragement.*

CONTENTS

Title Page
Copyright
Dedication
Introduction
CUSTOMER SERVICE
CHAPTER ONE	1
CHAPTER TWO	2
CHAPTER THREE	10
CHAPTER FOUR	12
CHAPTER FIVE	14
CHAPTER SIX	17
CHAPTER SEVEN	19
CHAPTER EIGHT	22
About The Author	25
Books By This Author	27

INTRODUCTION

In March 2024 the story of a customer's review of a Tomato paste on social media and the court case that ensued got tongues wagging.

I am not here to apportion blame. But I want to use this story to underline the importance of customer service, especially in this internet age, where one can reach billions from the keyboard of a smartphone.

Businesses are struggling; some are shutting down while others are smiling at the bank. No matter the state of the economy people must eat, go to school, travel, etcetera.

In this book, we will explore customer service and explain why it is the foundation for business success. A careful study of thriving businesses will reveal that customer focus is their business strategy. From employment to technology decisions, the customer decides.

How?

With their purchases.

Except you are selling addictive products like crack cocaine you must put customers first if you want to grow a successful business.

CUSTOMER SERVICE

FOR

BUSINESS SUCCESS

CHAPTER ONE

WHO IS A CUSTOMER?

An African proverb says a man's head cannot be shaved in his absence.
A common factor in any business is the customer.
Without the customer as the foundation and focus of the business, the business is on shaky ground.

WHO IS A CUSTOMER
1. A person or organization who buys goods or services from a shop or business. For example a client in a law firm.

2. A person or organization of a specified kind with whom one has to deal, such as a government official conducting a tax audit.
So a customer is
A person who buys goods or services from a shop
A person who can prevent people from buying goods and services from a shop by giving negative publicity.
The source of a company's revenue, profit, survival, or demise.
People who play a crucial role in driving demand and influencing market trends.

CHAPTER TWO

TYPES OF CUSTOMER

There are various types of customers. This list is not exhaustive.

1. POTENTIAL CUSTOMERS

A potential customer is a prospect who has shown interest in your product or service but has not bought yet. He is sniffing around with his funds. A car dealership should expect a lot of potential customers because of the high value of their goods and the necessity of a means of transport.

STEPS IN MANAGING POTENTIAL CUSTOMERS

1. Lead generation

Identify potential customers by marketing daily. Coca cola sells in billions but they still advertise everywhere.

Use social media, create content, network with others, and place social media advertisements.

2. Determine if the potential customer meets your ideal customer profile and has a genuine need for your product or service.

3. Engage

This is key.

Initiate contact and build relationships throughout PERSONALISED communication. Always use their names when available.

Address their needs and concerns politely. Let them know your product or service can meet their expectations.

Under promise and over-deliver.

4. Nurturing

Give them valuable information about your product and services.

Educate your potential customers. Provide verifiable testimonials from satisfied customers if you have.

5. Follow-up
Stay in touch regularly to remain on their minds. Answer all questions and be available to answer all questions. No question is trivial.
Provide means of communication, a telephone number, and an email, and ensure you are available to respond to inquiries. An unpicked call from a customer is a sign your business is not ready for prompt service.

6. Conversation
When the customer is ready to make a purchase make it as PAINLESS as possible.

7. Feedback and Retention
Get post-sale feedback from customers to ensure customer satisfaction, loyalty, and referrals.

2. FIRST-TIME CUSTOMERS
They are individuals and organizations buying from your business for the first time. Managing them effectively will lead to repeat business and referrals.

STEPS IN MANAGING FIRST-TIME CUSTOMERS
1. Welcome Experience
Ensure the first interaction with your business is welcoming and positive.
Ensure friendly greetings, easy navigation of your Website or store, and clear communication of your product or service.

2. On-boarding Process
Provide a smooth onboarding process that guides them in using your products and services where necessary.

3. Personalization

Use their names, if you know their preferences apply where possible.

4. Clear communication
Let them know what to expect from your products and services. Your fliers should be written in simple language. It's not meant to show off your level of education. Don't hide funny clauses in your contracts. Give a money-back guarantee. Why? It shows your confidence in your product.

5. Feedback Collection
Get feedback after their initial purchase to ensure the experience exceeds or at least equals expectations. If not find out why and ENHANCE your offering.
Don't cling to your product or service. Modify when necessary. This is not an ego trip. Don't become obsolete from stubbornness.

High-performing companies improve daily. The kdp.amazon.com account I opened has transformed. What does that tell me? They are working round-the-clock to make it a better experience for me in my publishing journey. Countries with low GDP are synonymous with poor technological advancement and product stagnation.

6. Special Offers
You could give first-time Customers discounts, promotions, or discounts on bulk purchases.

7. Customer Support
Have staff on the ground offer after-sales services. Prompt and helpful support can make a big difference in your business perception.

3. REPEAT CUSTOMERS
These are individuals who made more than one purchase from your business.
They are valuable to a business because they are the major contributors to the revenue of a company through continued

patronage. They are also a source of referrals for your business.

STEPS IN MANAGING REPEAT CUSTOMERS

1. Personalized Communication: Use their name and any relevant details you've gathered about their preferences.

2. Customer Loyalty Programs: This could include exclusive discounts, special offers for returning customers, and conversion referral commissions.

3. Feedback and Listening: Regularly seek and use feedback from repeat customers to understand their ever-changing needs and preferences. Feedback could come as complaints. Customer complaints are also a means of knowing what your competitors are offering.

4. Exceptional Customer Service: Address any issues promptly and go the extra mile to resolve problems to their satisfaction. This leads to customer loyalty.

5. Exclusive Offers and Benefits: Offer benefits to repeat customers. Give them access to test new products and give feedback.

6. Stay Connected: Stay in touch with your customers through your website and official newsletters.

7. Surprise and Delight Loyal Customers: Occasionally surprise repeat customers with unexpected gifts. It could be as simple as sending emails on their birthdays and special dates. Imagine an event planner who remembers to send a wedding anniversary message to her client. It could lead to a referral. Big companies have to find novel ways of making their customers feel special.

8. Build a Community: Create a niche of community around your brand. A repeat customer should feel valued and in the right place.

9. Monitor Customer Behavior: Are your customer's tastes changing? Are they still buying but have changed their method of buying? For example, if you have a restaurant and sales are

dropping it could be because you don't do takeaways and the trend is moving towards takeaways.

4. INTERNAL CUSTOMERS

Internal customers refer to individuals or departments within an organization who rely on the products, services, or information provided by another department to perform their jobs effectively. Unlike external customers who are outside the organization, internal customers are part of the same company or entity.

An organization's Internal Customer Service is a reflection of its external customer service.

STEPS IN MANAGING INTERNAL CUSTOMERS

1. Identifying Internal Customers: Understand which departments or individuals depend on the outputs of your department to perform their tasks.

2. Understanding Their Needs and Expectations: Communicate with internal customers to know their requirements, challenges, and expectations regarding the products, services, or information your department provides.

3. Customer Service Orientation: There must be a customer service mindset towards internal customers, treating them with professionalism, respect, and responsiveness. Set service standards for internal customer service, like deadlines to respond to inquiries between departments.

4. Effective Communication: Maintain clear and open communication channels with internal customers to ensure they know about your department's capabilities, timelines, and any changes that may impact them.

5. Quality and Timeliness: Deliver products, services, or information that meet or exceed internal customer expectations

for quality, accuracy, and timeliness.

6. Problem Resolution: Quickly address any issues or concerns by internal customers, demonstrating a commitment to resolving problems and improving processes.
Internal customer service is sometimes overlooked.

Sometimes staff from different departments see themselves as competitors thereby engaging in unnecessary battles causing the business service failure and loss of revenue. Making ALL departments focus on the paying customer could reduce interdepartmental conflict.

Internal customer service is key.

All internal staff regardless of department should focus on the customer- Who is king.
The MD/CEO might be on the top of the organization's organogram but the customer is actually the boss of everyone and is calling the shots. He can fire everyone by refusing to BUY.

5. DISSATISFIED CUSTOMERS

Dissatisfied customers are individuals who are unhappy or unsatisfied with a product, service, or experience provided by a company.
A dissatisfied customer is a gem.

How?
1. They complained to you, giving you a golden opportunity to make amends. They could have taken the business to your competitors reducing your revenue.

2. They may have identified a gap or weakness in your product or services you didn't identify.

3. By solving their problems you are avoiding future customer complaints.

4. They help you create a better version of your product or

services.

Dissatisfied customers are crucial for maintaining customer loyalty, reputation, and overall business success.

STEPS IN MANAGING DISSATISFIED CUSTOMERS

1. Listen Actively: Allow the customer to express their concerns fully without interrupting. Show empathy and understanding of their perspective. This is not a time to defend your product or service. Put yourself in your customer's shoes.

2. Apologize from your Heart: Even if the issue isn't directly your fault, apologize for the inconvenience or dissatisfaction the customer has experienced.

3. Agree the problem Exists: Acknowledge the issue the customer is facing is real and regrettable. Repeat their concerns to ensure you understand the situation correctly.

4. Take Responsibility: Accept the fault for any mistakes or shortcomings. Avoid blaming others or making excuses. Make amends by:

5. Offer Solutions: Propose various means of resolving the problem at no extra cost to the customer. This could be a refund or replacement.

6. Give Employees Authority: Give frontline employees the authority and tools to resolve customer issues timely without needing to escalate to higher levels causing more pain to the dissatisfied customer.

7. Follow Through: Ensure that promises made to the customer, such as callbacks, refunds, or replacements are implemented.

8. Learn and Improve: Use feedback from dissatisfied customers as an opportunity to identify areas for improvement in products, services, or processes.

9. Maintain Professionalism: Remain calm, patient, and

professional throughout the interaction, even if the customer becomes upset or angry.

10. Monitor and Analyze: Track customer complaints and feedback to identify recurring issues or trends that require systemic improvements.

11. Identify the Source of the Complaint: Is it technical or staff? If technical, resolve with appropriate technology. If staff, retrain immediately and monitor. If staff remains a source of customer complaints disengage immediately. You can't keep a staff antagonizing your customers, reducing your revenue, profitability, and business survival.

Resolving customer complaints well leads to customer satisfaction and loyalty. A business without excellent customer service is like a cake without icing.

CHAPTER THREE

WHAT IS A BUSINESS

A business is an organization created to do the following

1. Satisfaction for the customer
2. Profit for the owners
3. Taxes for government

Every business is created to solve a problem. Except you are selling addictives you should focus on your customer's satisfaction.

There are other reasons but these are the basics.

Most businesses put number two first, causing a lot of foundational issues.
You cannot make a profit in the long run from dissatisfied customers.
The short run maybe.
But in the long run.
It's a No No

This is the reason many businesses fail.
They open to make a profit.
This limits their creativity.

Other businesses avoid number 3 which is a crime and a legal issue.
It's also a spiritual issue because in the Bible Jesus said give unto Ceaser what belongs to Ceaser.
In Matt 17:27 Christ paid tax.

However, this lecture is focused on number one.

Because without number the one reason for business existence the next two are mirages.

CHAPTER FOUR

WHAT IS A SUCCESSFUL BUSINESS

A successful business meets these reasons for business creation.

That is

1. Customer Satisfaction:
Meeting customer needs effectively leads to repeat business, positive word of mouth, and customer loyalty.

2. Profitability:
Generate revenue that exceeds expenses leading to net profit and protecting business capital.

3. Adherence to Legal and ethical standards:
Which includes paying taxes and protecting the natural ecosystem.

4. Operational efficiency:
This helps businesses minimize costs, streamline processes, and deliver goods and services promptly in a conducive environment.

5. Talented and Motivated Employees:
These are the people who will deliver excellent customer service. Hiring, training, motivating, and retaining quality staff is a key to business success.

They also ensure the next point.

6. Innovation:
New, cheaper, and better ways to meet and exceed customer needs and satisfaction

7. Leadership and Succession:

Leadership is direction.
Succession is the future direction.

CHAPTER FIVE

WHAT IS CUSTOMER SERVICE

Customer service is the means of solving customer's needs by delivering goods and services to them. Customer service involves answering inquiries, delivering goods or services, and resolving customer complaints, Customer service is done through various channels such as phone, email, chat, or in-person interactions. Good customer service will meet the customer through the channel they prefer. However, some organizations force customers into a channel inconvenient for them. So what happens? They have opened the door for their competitors to service their customers who refused to move to the new channel. Good customer service aims to build positive relationships with customers and enhance their overall experience with the company by putting their customers FIRST.

Customer services are activities geared towards ensuring customers have positive emotions from engaging with an organization.

Customer service handles human emotions. Feelings are real. We smile, cry, frown, and more. When you ensure customers feel good across all platforms they engage with your business then you are on track to business survival and growth.

Don't wait for customer feedback. Actively seek customer feedback once they purchase from you.
For example when people pass a bank and smile at well-tended flower beds and neat premises.
Simply put-Customer service is customer focus.

Not product focus.

DANGERS OF PRODUCT-FOCUSED COMPANIES
1. STAGNATION
2. EXTINCTION
3. LIQUIDATION

4.

This is because customer tastes, demographics, needs, and desires…change.
An African proverb says you don't watch a masquerade dance by standing in one place. You move as the masquerade moves.

Looking at innovative countries and companies their GDPs and standard of living are high, whereas countries with obsolete products remain in the past.

Don't be satisfied with your product and services because there is always room for improvement.
Enter management meeting with the zeal to do more for your customer than any of your competition and charge employees to come out with novel ideas to meet customer expectations and your innovations in your industry will give you a cutting edge. Before your competition catches up you have moved on,
The first time I saw the BlackBerry phone I shuddered. The keypad was so tiny I wondered why the company approved the prototype for mass production. I expected a better version of the product but now the company is history.

Every time I become proud about my services I look at my Blackberry and come down from my high horse.

Yes, I still have it.
It's my reality check.
Let's look at cars.
Their functionality.
In the past a customer who said he doesn't like driving and wants

a car that can drive itself would be considered irrational.
Now cars are driving themselves.

Now you don't need to type. Several applications will convert your speech to text. Will it end there?
I don't think so.
Soon applications might convert thoughts to text.

Do you see how customer complaints and customer-focused companies drive innovation and technology?
Don't be left out.

A popular Igbo adage says the future is pregnant.
Let it birth customer-focused products and solutions.

This would improve customer satisfaction and business profitability. It would also generate employment opportunities to meet customers' demands.

CHAPTER SIX
WHAT A CUSTOMER IS NOT

A customer is NOT
 An interruption
A distraction
A waste of time
A complainant
A busy body
A person to quarrel with
A person to scam
A person to judge
A person to fleece

We should repeat this always to keep focused on satisfying our customers.
Analyze your wait time. Put yourself in your customer's shoes. If you had to wait for service that long will you or take your business elsewhere?

Let's look at a restaurant. You know your peak time. What stops you from hiring extra hands just for that peak time?

Analyze EVERYTHING that irritates your customer or you could birth and strengthen your competition.

I know of a bank with terrible customer service, although their management said otherwise.

What happened?
Their competitor bought land beside, opposite, or close to them and opened mega branches.

I don't want to give names but smile whenever I pass them sitting side by side.

The customer-insensitive bank keep cutting costs to keep their head out of water but their services are still terrible.

I tried to get an ATM card from them and was told to return the next day as their system was down. Their competitor has ATM card dispensing machines.

Yes, I still bank with them. I want to see if their customer service will ever improve.

CHAPTER SEVEN

FIVE DRIVERS OF CUSTOMER SERVICE

Note I am looking at this from the customer's perspective.
Why?
Because I believe businesses are open to satisfy customers. Any business activity that is not geared toward customers' needs and wants is an additional cost, and it's unfair for businesses to transfer such cost to customers via price.

1. RELIABILITY
This is a core driver. Does your product or service deliver results in a timely manner?
A story was told about an Igbo businessman. He was lying in a hospital bed with wires and, a drip line, and his wife was weeping, holding his hand, and praying feverishly. He had been there for several days. His shop boys were trying to keep brave faces. His survival key to their settlement after their contractual apprenticeship with him. When he opened his eyes, he responded to the shout of joy with a frown. "Why is everybody here?" He asked, "Who is in the shop?"
They stared at him in shock

"Common disappear, before I blink!" He ordered in a hoarse voice.

I laughed when I heard the story. This story underscores the importance of reliability in customer service satisfaction. Businesses should ensure it is available on all channels. It may take a while for a small business to get to that level but the internet has made it possible at a lower cost.

A website is advisable to improve reliability and visibility.

For example, if you are selling medicine for Malaria is your product effective?

If you have a restaurant, is your delivery fast and efficient? Do you open on time? I saw a post on X. The writer wanted those who sell bean balls to know they are critical. They should always open because of the agony of not getting his fix of bean balls when he needs them. This underscores reliability.

2. TANGIBLES

This refers to the physical business premises and communication documents like fliers.

Is the premise neat and well-painted? I went to a supermarket and their shopping carts were black with dirt. I asked for the manager immediately because those shopping carts were health hazards.

The cleaners in an organization should hate dirt to do a thorough job.

Are employees well dressed and smiling? Are they wearing their identity cards? Is the temperature okay? Colors play a role in identifying your business. Colors also affect customer's emotions. Some colors are calming others evoke joy. Think carefully before you settle on the colors you want for your business.

A lot can be done under tangibles.

3. ASSURANCE

This is the credibility and ability of staff. Customers must feel workers can deliver the business products and services. So train and retrain your staff to be the best in your industry.

For example: in a tailoring business, staff must sew styles picked by customers.

4. EMPATHY

Customers must feel the business is acting solely in the interest of the customers.

This is key. The business must not make the customer feel they are a balance sheet item. They must make the customers feel their staff is acting in their interest. That's the secret of customer

service, especially during service recovery.
Successful businesses make the customer feel like royalty during every interaction.

5. RESPONSIVENESS

This is how fast the business reacts to customer inquiries or complaints.

Businesses should remember we are in a digital age. A customer can complain on Facebook and expect the organization to respond. If a bank changes its software and its customers can't do transfers from their phones the head of information technology still has his job. It shows how unresponsive the bank is. No matter the advantages the change will give the internal processes of the bank the headache it will give customers should be considered.

Don't think your customer is asking too much.

A customer who tells you he wants to buy a car that will drive itself might seem insane, but some cars are driving themselves now. Customer complaints are future technology.

Don't assume your clients can bear the inconvenience of your in-house shortcomings. Litigations can arise from customer service failures. Even if the company wins the litigation, the negative publicity should be avoided.

Management must improve on these drivers of customer service daily. As long as these drivers keep improving, customer satisfaction which leads to customer loyalty will improve.

Revenue inflow from satisfied customers is what makes a business successful. Unless an organization sells addictive products like Heroin, it can't avoid customer service.

CHAPTER EIGHT
CASE STUDY

Sales have crashed in a Supermarket.
Located is close to three large estates.
A quick investigation showed that sales dropped because a new Supermarket opened opposite them selling everything on their shelves and more.
They have a larger parking space.
They also have a restaurant, a bakery, and a saloon.
They also poached two of their friendly cashiers. Their aisles were spacious and their lighting modern, their air conditioning chilled. What should be done to reverse this trend using our knowledge of drivers of customer service?

RELIABILITY
They opened on time but should have included a bakery, restaurant, and saloon before their competitor.

TANGIBLES
They need to upgrade their supermarket. Make the aisles spacious, temperature cool.
In the end, their supermarket should look and feel better than their competitors.

ASSURANCE
They should train and retrain their staff to give the best service.

EMPATHY
Allowing unfriendly staff to remain on their payroll is an indictment on management. Staff must be caring and friendly while attending to customers.

They should find out why their friendly cashiers were poached so easily and correct the problem. The owner may need to improve the welfare of his staff. Their competitors gave higher pay or better incentives.

Management should use rewards and recognition to improve staff performance. Staff appraisal should be conducted to foster acceptable behavior and eliminate toxic behavior.

Staff and technology deliver customer service.

RESPONSIVENESS
Take customer complaints seriously. Some may have complained about the unfriendly staff and nothing was done.
Customer-focused businesses should conduct mystery shopping regularly. This would observe the organization with fresh, unbiased eyes.
The feedback from the mystery shopping exercise must be used to make corrections and grow the business.
In this scenario, the Supermarket has to implement strategies to win its customers back immediately.
CONCLUSION
Products exist because customers exit.
Never forget that.

ABOUT THE AUTHOR

Awele Onwuka

Awele is a trained accountant with passion for business growth through service.
As a business coach she loves to see businesses start, grow, and succeed.
She is also an author with several books on sale.

BOOKS BY THIS AUTHOR

Ugo: Travails Of The Girl Child

Ugo wonders why her life is difficult because of her gender. She is intelligent and tries to make the best out of her situation. Events unfold, plunging her into more trouble, making her take drastic action.

Chiemela: Travails Of The Girl Child 1

The female gender before birth is under attack, with hurdles to overcome to thrive. Sadly the vicious circle is passed from mother to daughter from generation to generation. Chiemela terrified of her father, tries to survive each day. A critical loss worsens her situation, exposing her to danger.

Color Of Hope

Nma leaves her father's house for her new home with Chike. She expects a smooth ride. Infertility and domestic violence from an unlikely source put her marriage at risk.

Online Publishing An Eye Opener

Learn how to self-publish your books online, fast, and make an income.

www.ingramcontent.com/pod-product-compliance
Lightning Source LLC
Chambersburg PA
CBHW070956220526
45471CB00007B/3058